NEW YORK
GIANTS

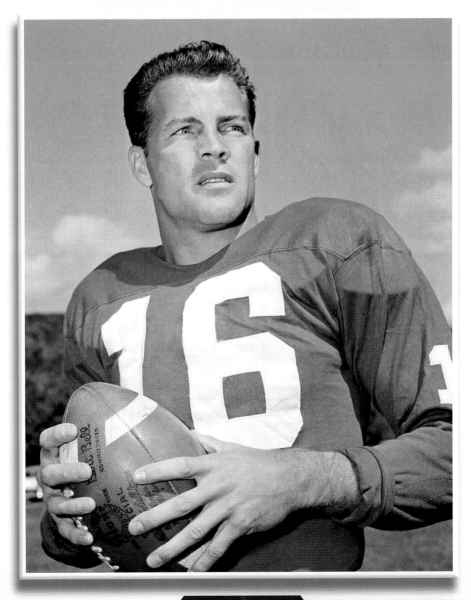

by Marty Gitlin

Published by ABDO Publishing Company, 8000 West 78th Street, Edina, Minnesota 55439. Copyright © 2011 by Abdo Consulting Group, Inc. International copyrights reserved in all countries. No part of this book may be reproduced in any form without written permission from the publisher. SportsZone™ is a trademark and logo of ABDO Publishing Company.

Printed in the United States of America,
North Mankato, Minnesota
062010
092010

 THIS BOOK CONTAINS AT LEAST 10% RECYCLED MATERIALS.

Editor: Matt Tustison
Copy Editor: Nicholas Cafarelli
Interior Design and Production: Kazuko Collins
Cover Design: Becky Daum

Photo Credits: David Stluka/AP Images, cover; AP Images, title page, 7, 12, 14, 17, 18, 21, 22, 25, 26, 31, 33, 42 (top), 42 (middle), 42 (bottom); Amy Sancetta/AP Images, 4, 43 (top); Reed Saxon/AP Images, 8; Eric Risberg/AP Images, 11; NFL Photos/AP Images, 28; Charlie Riedel/AP Images, 34, 43 (bottom); Bill Waugh/AP Images, 37, 43 (middle); David Duprey/AP Images, 38, 41; Bill Kostroun/AP Images, 44, 47

Library of Congress Cataloging-in-Publication Data
Gitlin, Marty.
 New York Giants / Marty Gitlin.
   p. cm. — (Inside the NFL)
 Includes index.
 ISBN 978-1-61714-021-1
 1. New York Giants (Football team—History—Juvenile literature. I. Title.
 GV956.N4G58 2010
 796.332'64097471—dc22
                          2010017369

TABLE OF CONTENTS

CHAPTER 1

GREATEST TEAM
IN HISTORY?

The New York Giants had always been a proud franchise. But a bit of that pride went away with each losing season.

There was not much pride left as the mid-1980s approached. The Giants' most recent teams had been okay but were not championship quality. New York had played the role of punching bag for National Football League (NFL) opponents through much of the prior two decades.

Longtime owner Wellington Mara had grown impatient. In 1983, he promoted untested

THE 3–4 DEFENSE

One reason for the incredible success of the Giants' defense under coach Bill Parcells was his installation of the 3–4 alignment. This defensive setup features three linemen and four linebackers. Though a few teams had experimented with the 3–4 over the years, nearly every defense used four defensive linemen up front and three linebackers behind them. Parcells was instrumental in popularizing the 3–4. Many teams use this defense today. It is intended to allow the three defensive linemen to engage the offensive linemen and free up the linebackers to make tackles.

QUARTERBACK PHIL SIMMS AND OFFENSIVE TACKLE BRAD BENSON CELEBRATE DURING THE GIANTS' 39–20 VICTORY OVER THE BRONCOS IN SUPER BOWL XXI ON JANUARY 25, 1987.

TERRIFIC TAYLOR

When fans debate the finest linebacker to ever play football, one of the names that gets mentioned is Lawrence Taylor.

Taylor recorded more than 10 sacks in seven seasons in a row starting in 1984. He had a league-high 20.5 in the championship year of 1986. His quickness and intensity forced opposing coaches to change their game plans. These attempts to prevent him from dominating their offenses usually did not work.

He achieved a rare feat in 1986 when he was selected as the NFL Most Valuable Player (MVP). That award is usually given to quarter-backs and running backs.

"You saw hunger," said San Francisco 49ers Hall of Fame quarterback Joe Montana. "Some guys were great playing their position but didn't have that feeling inside, and that was something [Taylor] had with him every down of every game, and he never lost it."

defensive coordinator Bill Parcells to head coach. The move appeared to backfire right away. A team that had been somewhat successful the previous two seasons went 3–12–1 in Parcells's first season as coach.

But suddenly the Giants blossomed. The team's defense improved rapidly. The offense found a spark in new starting quarterback Phil Simms. The Giants reached the second round of the playoffs in 1984 and 1985. In 1986, they appeared ready for greatness.

Linebackers Lawrence Taylor, Harry Carson, and Carl Banks and defensive end Leonard Marshall were the standouts on one of the best

THE GIANTS' LAWRENCE TAYLOR HAD 20.5 SACKS IN THE 1986 SEASON AND WAS NAMED THE NFL'S MVP. HE WAS PART OF A FEROCIOUS NEW YORK DEFENSE.

defenses in the NFL. Aside from the first game and the last, the Giants surrendered no more than 20 points in any contest in the 1986 regular season. It ended with nine victories in a row and a 14–2 record. New York won the National Football Conference (NFC) East Division by two games.

The Giants' offense was merely mediocre through most of 1986. But when the playoffs approached, it came to life. The Giants averaged just 20.3 points in their first 12 games. They scored 17 points or fewer in five of those games. In their final four regular-season games, they clicked for 31.8 points per game. This included 55 points in clobbering the Green Bay Packers in the season finale.

The Giants continued to play very well in the postseason. They earned the first Super Bowl berth in team history with a 49–3 win over the San Francisco 49ers and a 17–0 shutout of the Washington Redskins. The Giants held the 49ers and the Redskins to a combined 374 yards, 21 first downs, and 69 rushing yards on 36 carries.

All that separated the Giants from a world championship were the Denver Broncos.

GIANTS QUARTERBACK PHIL SIMMS WAS ALMOST FLAWLESS IN SUPER BOWL XXI. HE WENT 22–FOR–25 FOR 268 YARDS AND THREE TOUCHDOWNS.

Simms rose to the occasion in Super Bowl XXI on January 25, 1987, in Pasadena, California. He was nearly perfect, completing 22 of 25 passes for 268 yards and three touchdowns. He was named the game's MVP. The Giants won 39–20. During the wild celebration in the locker room after the triumph, Parcells raved about his quarterback. Simms had been criticized for past playoff performances.

"That's as good as Phil has ever played," Parcells said. "This dispelled for the last time any myths about Phil Simms. He was absolutely magnificent today."

So were his teammates. Eight different receivers caught at least one pass from Simms. Tight end Mark Bavaro, who had been the team's top receiver all

SUPER JOE

Running back Joe Morris was a key to the 1986 Giants' Super Bowl run. He rushed for 1,829 yards and 18 touchdowns in 19 games. His performance earned him a spot on the NFC Pro Bowl team for the second consecutive year. Morris, however, did not enjoy long-term success. He broke a foot before the 1989 season and was never the same.

season, snagged a 13-yard scoring strike that put the Giants ahead to stay.

Mara had found a gem in Parcells. The Giants were about to begin an era of greatness that brought back memories of the team's glory days.

NEW YORK COACH BILL PARCELLS IS CARRIED OFF THE FIELD AFTER HIS TEAM'S VICTORY IN SUPER BOWL XXI IN PASADENA, CALIFORNIA.

CHAPTER 2

AN EARLY NFL POWERHOUSE

I

n 1925, New York businessman Tim Mara purchased the Giants for $500. Could he have possibly imagined that in 2006 the value of the franchise would be placed at $890 million?

It is quite unlikely, particularly since he lost $40,000 with his investment in 1926. But Mara, who owned the Giants until he sold them to son Wellington in 1959, had to be applauding their performance on the field. They were among the best teams in the young NFL.

The Giants began gaining a reputation for a strong defense from the start. In 1927, they had

10 shutouts in 13 games to lead the team to an 11–1–1 record

DISASTER AVOIDED

The Giants were threatened with extinction in 1925. Owner Tim Mara had lost an estimated $40,000 and needed a huge attendance in the last home game of the season to save the team. Fortunately for Mara and the Giants, star running back Red Grange was in town with his Chicago Bears. More than 70,000 people paid their way into the Polo Grounds. The huge crowd gave Mara money and hope that New York could indeed support an NFL team.

GIANTS CENTER MEL HEIN RECEIVES A WATCH FROM NFL PRESIDENT JOSEPH CARR ON DECEMBER 11, 1938, FOR BEING SELECTED AS THE LEAGUE'S MVP.

TIM MARA WAS THE FOUNDER OF THE NEW YORK GIANTS. HE PAID A $500 FRANCHISE FEE IN ORDER FOR THE GIANTS TO JOIN THE NFL IN 1925.

LEGEND'S SHORT STAY

Perhaps the greatest athlete in history performed for the Giants. Born on an American Indian reservation in Oklahoma, Jim Thorpe blossomed into an Olympic champion. He also became a professional baseball and football player. He joined the Giants for just three games at the end of his career in their first season in 1925.

and its first championship. Winning quickly became a habit. The Giants suffered just three losing seasons through 1944. They played in eight title games in the process.

Perhaps the most noteworthy season was in 1934.

The Giants finished with an average 8–5 record. They scored 17 points or fewer in all but one game and were considered an unworthy title game opponent for Chicago. After all, the Bears had won 13 contests in a row.

The gloom and doom predicted for the Giants appeared justified when they fell behind the Bears 13–3. A freezing rain had turned the Giants' home field, the Polo Grounds, into a slippery mess. Equipment manager Abe Cohen found basketball sneakers for his players at halftime. The improved traction allowed the Giants to score 27 straight points in the fourth quarter. They emerged with a 30–13 win that is now known as "The Sneakers Game."

"They were slipping and sliding," said Giants quarterback Harry Newman, describing the Bears' failed attempts to tackle

his sneaker-wearing teammates in the fourth quarter. "They couldn't touch anybody."

Another gratifying year was 1938. The Giants surrendered 41 points in losing two of their first three games. After that, they allowed just 38 in going unbeaten the rest of the regular season, finishing 8–2–1. They gave up only 10 points in their last five games to set up a clash for the title with Green Bay.

The Packers were ahead 17–16 when Giants running back Hank Soar led his team down the field. He carried the ball five times and added a reception to

STANDOUT PLAYER, COACH

Steve Owen did not leave the Giants after spending six years with them as one of the NFL's best defensive tackles. He began coaching the team full time in 1931 and ended up in the Pro Football Hall of Fame.

Owen captained the 1927 title team. But when he took over as coach, his legend grew. He stayed on the job for 23 years.

The Giants enjoyed their greatest run of success during Owen's time as coach. He guided them to eight division crowns and two NFL championships while posting a record of 151–100–17.

He also proved innovative. He established the two-platoon system. Players usually competed on both offense and defense. But Owen created a system of specialization in which his players remained fresher by playing only one or the other.

Owen was enshrined in the Hall of Fame in 1966.

move the Giants into position to score. Then he leaped to grab a pass from quarterback Ed Danowski and dragged a tackler into the end zone for the winning score. The Giants became the first team to win two NFL Championship Games.

New York experienced its share of frustration, however. The Giants lost showdowns for the league crown in 1933, 1935, 1939, 1941, 1944, and 1946. The team would remain strong into the 1950s. But it would not win another title until 1956. That year, the Giants earned one of the most dominant championship game victories in the history of the NFL.

NEW YORK QUARTERBACK FRANK FILCHOCK AND COACH STEVE OWEN LOOK ON DURING THE GIANTS' 24–14 LOSS TO THE BEARS IN THE 1946 NFL CHAMPIONSHIP GAME.

CHAPTER 3

WIN SOME, LOSE SOME

The Giants of the early 1950s experienced the same scenario as the team did in previous decades. That is, they would play well, but not well enough to reach the playoffs. Or they would reach the doorstep of an NFL title, but the door most often would be slammed in their faces.

The team had lost its last four championship games heading into the new decade. In 1950, the trend continued. The Giants reached the playoffs with a 10–2 record. But they fell to the Cleveland Browns in a one-game playoff to decide which team would advance to the NFL Championship Game. And few were

LEGENDARY LOMBARDI

Arguably the greatest head coach in NFL history learned the tools of the trade with the Giants. Vince Lombardi specialized in running New York's offense from 1954 to 1958. He went on to become the head coach of the Green Bay Packers in their glory days of the early and mid-1960s. His teams won the first two Super Bowls. Today, the Super Bowl trophy is called the Vince Lombardi Trophy.

COACH JIM LEE HOWELL AND RUNNING BACK FRANK GIFFORD CELEBRATE THE GIANTS' 47–7 ROUT OF THE BEARS IN THE 1956 NFL TITLE GAME.

RENAISSANCE MAN

Hank Soar was a running back/defensive back who played for the Giants from 1937 to 1944 and then again in 1946. He had the winning touchdown catch for New York in its 23–17 victory over the Green Bay Packers in the 1938 NFL Championship Game.

Soar did more than dabble in other sports. He participated in professional basketball and baseball after his football career—though not as a player.

In the late 1940s, he coached the Providence Steamrollers of the Basketball Association of America, which changed into the National Basketball Association (NBA). And from 1950 to the late 1970s, he served as a Major League Baseball umpire, working American League games. He was the first base umpire in the only perfect game in World Series history, pitched by the New York Yankees' Don Larsen in 1956.

shocked when they recorded winning marks in four of the next five years without qualifying for the postseason. The Giants, however, were compiling a star-studded roster.

The offense featured tackle Roosevelt Brown. He came aboard in 1953 and was named to the All-NFL team eight straight seasons. Halfback Frank Gifford, who also played as a receiver and a defensive back, was chosen to eight Pro Bowls. He racked up 9,862 total yards in his career and as of 2010 still held the Giants' record with 78 touchdowns. Charlie Conerly also emerged as one of the most reliable quarterbacks in the league.

OFFENSIVE TACKLE ROOSEVELT BROWN, SHOWN IN 1958, PLAYED FOR THE GIANTS FROM 1953 TO 1965. HE WAS ENSHRINED IN THE PRO FOOTBALL HALL OF FAME IN 1975.

22   NEW YORK GIANTS

Meanwhile, the defense maintained its strong reputation. Defensive end Andy Robustelli made five Pro Bowls with the Giants. Defensive back Emlen Tunnell set a team mark of 74 interceptions that as of 2010 still stood.

With several future Pro Football Hall of Famers leading the way, the Giants remained strong. But nothing seemed to have changed much in 1956. They did reach the playoffs. But they did not perform very well down the stretch in the regular season. The Bears had tormented them in previous title games. Chicago was expected to do the same when the teams clashed for the NFL championship at Yankee Stadium in New York.

But instead, it was the Giants who tormented the Bears. New York's offensive line opened huge holes for the running backs. Conerly tossed two touchdown passes. The defense, led by rookie linebacker Sam Huff, held Chicago to 67 rushing yards on 32 carries. The Giants raced to a 34–7 halftime lead and cruised to a 47–7 win for their first title since 1938.

ROUGH, TOUGH HUFF

Giants Hall of Fame linebacker Sam Huff is known as the only player to consistently stop the Cleveland Browns' Jim Brown. Brown is considered by many NFL experts to be the finest running back in league history. In one confrontation, Huff halted Brown on a play and said to him, "Brown, you stink." Huff stopped Brown again on the next play and said, "Brown, you still stink!" But on the following play, Brown faked Huff out and sprinted away for a 65-yard touchdown. "Hey, Huff," Brown yelled as he trotted back to the sideline. "How do I smell from here?"

VINCE LOMBARDI WAS AN ASSISTANT COACH IN CHARGE OF RUNNING THE GIANTS' OFFENSE FROM 1954 TO 1958. HE LATER BECAME A LEGENDARY HEAD COACH WITH THE PACKERS.

NO TITLE FOR TITTLE

One of the most successful quarterbacks to wear a Giants uniform owned the long name of Yelberton Abraham Tittle. It is no wonder he was known simply as Y. A. Tittle. The Giants traded for Tittle in 1961. He led the team to the playoffs in each of the next three years. His best performance came in 1963. He had 221 completions and set a single-season team record, which still stood through 2009, with 36 touchdown passes. He failed to win a championship. But he was inducted into the Pro Football Hall of Fame in 1971.

"Those linebackers were terrific," Bears receiver Harlon Hill said. "No matter which way I turned, there was a linebacker on me. They were better than us. That's all."

Two years later, the Giants would not be the better team in the NFL title game. They would, however, participate in what many consider the best game in the league's history.

The popularity of the league today is often traced back to the 1958 NFL Championship Game between the Giants and the Baltimore Colts at Yankee Stadium. A national television audience sat spellbound as the teams played to a 17–17 tie in regulation. They were forced to play overtime to decide the victor. The Colts won it on a 1-yard touchdown run by Alan Ameche. Hall of Fame quarterback Johnny Unitas engineered the winning 80-yard drive.

The Colts won the game. But the real winner was the NFL. The league had previously not been as popular as college football.

"One had to come away with the conclusion that the Colts-Giants blockbuster was one of the greatest spectacles in sport's history," wrote Morris Siegel of the *Washington Daily News*.

ALAN AMECHE'S 1-YARD TOUCHDOWN RUN GIVES THE COLTS A 23–17
OVERTIME WIN AGAINST THE GIANTS IN THE 1958 NFL TITLE GAME.

The Giants were not better than their opponent in the 1958 championship clash or in subsequent title games. After their 1956 championship season, the Giants compiled a regular-season record of 65–22–3 in the next seven years and qualified for the playoffs five times. But they scored just 50 points in five championship games and lost them all.

And soon they were to go from a contender to a struggling team.

CHAPTER 4

THE LONG, HARD ROAD

Perhaps it was the trade of superb linebacker Sam Huff to Washington. Perhaps it was the inability to find a suitable quarterback. Perhaps the Giants had been too good for too long and were simply due for a nosedive.

Perhaps it was a combination of many factors. But the bottom line is the Giants began to play bad football in 1964 and continued to play bad football through much of the 1970s.

The team nearly won the NFL title in 1963, falling by just four points to powerful Chicago in the championship game.

RUNNING IN CIRCLES

Maybe the most significant reason for the Giants' collapse in the 1960s was the lack of a running attack. The Giants could not find a productive rusher until Ron Johnson became their first 1,000-yard back in 1970. From 1962 to 1969, seven different backs led the team in rushing. And none of them gained more than 743 yards in a season. More amazing is that during the six-season period from 1964 to 1969, only one Giants back rushed for 100 yards or more in a game. Ernie Koy achieved that feat in 1967.

GIANTS COACH ALLIE SHERMAN INSTRUCTS QUARTERBACK Y. A. TITTLE DURING A GAME IN 1964. NEW YORK FINISHED JUST 2–10–2 THAT SEASON.

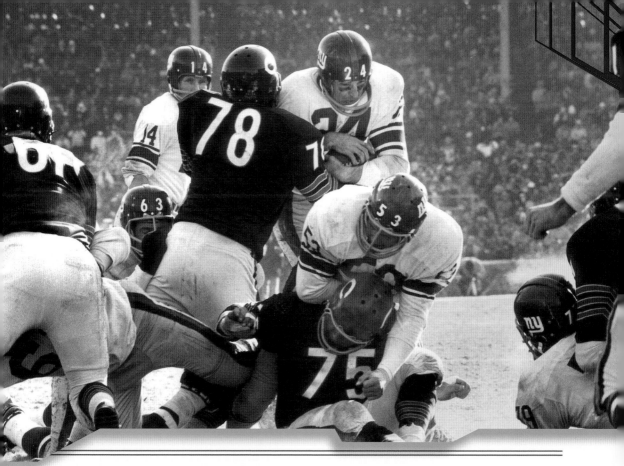

THE GIANTS' PHIL KING ATTEMPTS TO GAIN YARDAGE IN THE TEAM'S
14–10 LOSS TO THE BEARS IN THE 1963 NFL CHAMPIONSHIP GAME.

PLAY BALL!

The Giants shared stadiums with three different baseball teams from 1925 to 1975. For 30 years beginning in 1925, they played their games at the Polo Grounds, home of the National League New York Giants. They then switched to Yankee Stadium, home of the American League New York Yankees. Finally, they played one year at Shea Stadium, sharing that park with the National League New York Mets.

New York had a powerful offense in 1963. The team scored an NFL-high 448 points (an average of 32 per game), finished 11–3, and won the Eastern Conference. Quarterback Y. A. Tittle threw for 36 touchdowns, an NFL record at the time, against just 14 interceptions. Pro Bowl selections Del Shofner (64 catches for

1,181 yards) and Frank Gifford (42 catches for 657 yards) were Tittle's favorite targets.

The Giants' defense held up its end of the bargain as well. The unit was led by Huff. Cornerback Dick Lynch also was a key player. He made nine interceptions that season, returning three of them for touchdowns.

The Giants faced a tough, physical Bears team in the NFL Championship Game on December 29, 1963. The contest was held in frigid conditions at Wrigley Field in Chicago.

The Giants took a 7–0 lead thanks to a 14-yard touchdown pass from Tittle to Gifford. But Tittle battled a knee injury throughout the game. He had to sit out a few series. Chicago scored two touchdowns on short runs from quarterback Bill Wade. The Bears prevailed 14–10.

In 1964, the Giants fell to 2–10–2, the worst record in the team's history. And in 1966, they sunk even lower with a 1–12–1 mark.

The defense that had been a Giants trademark collapsed with the trade of Huff and the retirement of standout defensive end Andy Robustelli.

The Giants allowed just 280 points in winning the Eastern Conference in 1963. But they gave up 399 in 1964 and an alarming 501 in 1966.

The 1966 season included a 72–41 thrashing by Washington. During one five-week stretch late that season, the Giants surrendered an average of 50 points per game.

Coach Allie Sherman, who had guided the Giants to the playoffs in 1961, 1962, and 1963, survived the bad years.

SCRAMBLING FRAN

Most quarterbacks of the 1960s and early 1970s stood frozen like statues as they prepared to pass. If a defensive lineman or linebacker bore down on them, they were pretty much doomed to be sacked.

But not Fran Tarkenton, who played with the Giants from 1967 to 1971 and also spent many years with the Minnesota Vikings. In five seasons in New York, he threw for 13,905 yards and 103 touchdowns. But he also avoided sacks time and again.

The Giants paid a heavy price in 1967 to get Tarkenton from Minnesota, including two first-round draft picks.

"We needed a quarterback who could help us grow as a team," coach Allie Sherman said. "Francis has done that."

Tarkenton played a key role in the Giants finishing 7–7 that year after they had gone 1–12–1 in 1966.

He managed to raise the team back up to mediocrity. But when the Giants lost their final four games in 1968 and all five preseason games in 1969, he was fired and replaced by Alex Webster.

The new coach did no better. He guided New York to a 9–5 record in 1970. But he recorded two losing seasons in the next three. In 1973, the Giants fell to a disastrous 2–11–1 record.

The coaching carousel continued to turn. Bill Arnsparger replaced Webster in 1974. John McVay replaced Arnsparger in 1976. Ray Perkins replaced McVay in 1979.

FRAN TARKENTON WAS A STANDOUT QUARTERBACK FOR THE GIANTS FROM 1967 TO 1971. THE TEAM HAD A WINNING SEASON ONLY ONCE DURING THAT STRETCH, HOWEVER.

Fran Tarkenton, wide receiver Homer Jones, running back Ron Johnson, defensive back Willie Williams, and place-kicker Pete Gogolak.

But Tarkenton asked to be traded. He was dealt to the Minnesota Vikings before the 1972 season. The Giants suffered at that important position until Phil Simms arrived eight years later.

The 1986 Giants gave the team its first Super Bowl championship. An era of excellence was about to begin. And even after Simms and Parcells were gone, the Giants remained quite familiar with playing for world titles.

New York finally rebounded under Perkins and even reached the playoffs in 1981. It was the Giants' first playoff trip in 18 years. Still, the glory days did not return until Bill Parcells took over as coach.

The Giants of the lean years boasted some talented players. These included quarterback

PETE GOGOLAK PLAYED FOR THE GIANTS FROM 1966 TO 1974. HE WAS THE FIRST "SOCCER-STYLE" KICKER IN THE NFL.

CHAPTER 5

SURPRISE! THEY'RE IN THE SUPER BOWL

The history of the Giants can generally be broken into three eras: the period of excellence from 1925 to 1963, the lean years of 1964 to 1983, and the era of title contention from 1984 to the present.

The beginning of the last stage launched when the 1986 Giants won the team's first Super Bowl. The 1989 and the 1990 Giants also reached the postseason.

In 1990, the Giants won their first 10 games and allowed just 13.2 points per game. They defeated Chicago and San Francisco to return to the Super Bowl. The linebacker group, led by Lawrence Taylor, Carl Banks, and Pepper Johnson, was again the team's strength.

The Giants were forced to play for the NFL championship with backup quarterback

LONG, FUN RUN

The Giants went 13 years without suffering through consecutive losing seasons. Then they went 5–11 in 1995 and 6–10 in 1996. It was the first time they had losing records in back-to-back years since 1982 and 1983.

PLAXICO BURRESS BRINGS IN A GAME-WINNING 13-YARD TOUCHDOWN CATCH IN THE GIANTS' 17–14 VICTORY OVER THE PATRIOTS IN SUPER BOWL XLII.

WANT A WINNER? HIRE PARCELLS

Bill Parcells is the football fix-it man. Three struggling teams have hired him as coach. He transformed them all into winners.

After turning the Giants around in the 1980s, he took over a New England team that was coming off a 2–14 season in 1992. The 1994 Patriots made the playoffs. Two years later, Parcells led the team to the Super Bowl. He then quit and signed on as the New York Jets' coach and general manager. The Jets had finished a miserable 1–15 in 1996. Parcells guided them to a 9–7 record a year later. The next year, they reached the American Football Conference title game with a 12–4 mark. Parcells later followed the same path with the Dallas Cowboys. He took a team that had gone 5–11 and helped it earn two playoff berths.

Parcells is known for his gruff exterior and for criticizing his players at times to motivate them.

Jeff Hostetler. He had replaced injured starter Phil Simms. But Hostetler performed well. The Giants also received a strong game from running back Ottis Anderson. New York led the Buffalo Bills 20–19 with just four seconds remaining. Buffalo lined up for a potential game-winning field goal. When Bills kicker Scott Norwood's 47-yard field-goal attempt sailed wide to the right, the Giants were again champions.

When he awarded the Super Bowl trophy to his coach, Giants co-owner Tim Mara, a grandson of the original team owner, exclaimed, "Bill Parcells is the best coach the Giants have ever had."

THE BILLS' NATE ODOMES CANNOT PREVENT THE GIANTS' STEPHEN BAKER FROM MAKING A 14-YARD TOUCHDOWN RECEPTION IN NEW YORK'S 20–19 WIN IN SUPER BOWL XXV.

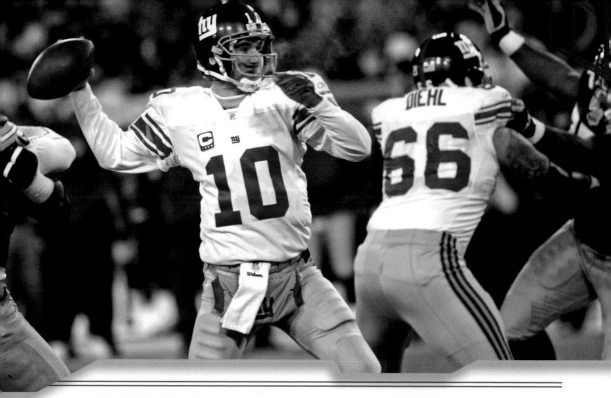

ELI MANNING PREPARES TO PASS DURING THE GIANTS' 23–20 OVERTIME
WIN AGAINST THE PACKERS IN THE NFC TITLE GAME IN JANUARY 2008.

Parcells retired after that season. The team struggled under replacement Ray Handley. The Giants had some success under subsequent coaches Dan Reeves and Jim Fassel.

In 2000, a Giants squad led by defensive end Michael Strahan, running back Tiki Barber, and wide receiver Amani Toomer routed Minnesota 41–0 to qualify for the team's third Super Bowl. This time, the Giants lost 34–7 to the Baltimore Ravens.

CRUNCH TIME

The Giants always had strong defensive teams during the regular season of Super Bowl years. That is, until 2007. The team that season surrendered 30 points or more five times and allowed an average of 21.9 points per game. But the defense began playing far better in the playoffs, giving up just 16.3 points per game against competition that included strong offensive teams in Dallas, Green Bay, and New England.

By the middle of the decade, a new cast of Giants was playing winning football under coach Tom Coughlin. Still, critics complained that they were not performing up to their potential.

The 2007 Giants barely reached the playoffs. Many awaited their quick elimination. The Giants responded by upsetting Tampa Bay, Dallas, and Green Bay to again qualify for the Super Bowl.

The Giants displayed a fierce defense in the postseason. Linemen Strahan, Justin Tuck, and Osi Umenyiora had combined for 32 of the team's whopping 52 quarterback sacks in the regular season.

Meanwhile, young quarterback Eli Manning, running back Brandon Jacobs, and receiver Plaxico Burress led a strong offense.

THE OTHER MANNING

Giants quarterback Eli Manning has an even more famous brother. Peyton Manning is the star quarterback of the Indianapolis Colts and arguably one of the best to ever play the position. Though it is unlikely Eli will ever be considered as talented as Peyton, he has continued to improve. He threw for 3,238 yards and 21 touchdowns in 2008 and a career-best 4,021 yards and 27 touchdowns in 2009.

The Giants had gotten hot at the right time. But awaiting them in the Super Bowl were the powerful New England Patriots. The Patriots were attempting to join the 1972 Miami Dolphins as the only teams in NFL history to complete an entire season, including the playoffs, undefeated. Most football fans and media members gave the Giants little chance to win.

The Giants did not care. They held the Patriots to 45 rushing yards. Burress caught a 13-yard touchdown pass from

Manning with 35 seconds left to give New York a stunning 17–14 victory. During the postgame celebration, Strahan spoke about the Giants proving that they deserved to be champions.

"We didn't do it to prove [critics] wrong," he exclaimed. "We did it to prove to ourselves that we could do it. We were stopping the best offense in football. Of course, they were surprised. We shocked the world. We shocked ourselves."

The Giants had been a contender again for 25 years. But there was no more satisfying championship than the one they earned that day.

Strahan retired after the Super Bowl-winning season. He played his entire 15-year career with the Giants. He had 141.5 sacks. This included an NFL-record 22.5 in 2001.

New York had another strong season in 2008, finishing 12–4 and winning the NFC East. However, the rival Philadelphia Eagles upset host New York 23–11 in the playoffs' divisional round. The Giants won their first five games in 2009 but slumped to an 8–8 finish and did not make the postseason.

New York, though, had Coughlin and Manning to lead the way into the future. The coach and the quarterback had already proven that they could succeed on the game's grandest stage. Indeed, big things still seemed in store for the Giants, one of the NFL's most celebrated teams.

THE GIANTS' MICHAEL STRAHAN CELEBRATES AFTER SACKING THE PATRIOTS' TOM BRADY IN SUPER BOWL XLII. NEW YORK DEFEATED PREVIOUSLY UNBEATEN NEW ENGLAND 17–14.

TIMELINE

1925	New York businessman Tim Mara purchases an NFL franchise for the city for $500. Mara loses $40,000 on the team. But the profits from a crowd of 70,000 watching the Giants play Red Grange and the Chicago Bears at the Polo Grounds on December 6 save the franchise.
1927	The Giants give up just 20 points all season and win their first NFL title with an 11–1–1 record.
1934	The Giants win "The Sneakers Game" by switching to basketball shoes after halftime. The 30–13 defeat of visiting Chicago on December 9 gives New York the NFL championship.
1938	A 23–17 home victory over the Green Bay Packers on December 11 produces another NFL title.
1950	The Giants lose 8–3 to the host Cleveland Browns in a divisional playoff game on December 17. It marks New York's sixth straight loss in a postseason game.
1956	The host Giants clobber the Bears 47–7 on December 30 to win the NFL crown.
1958	New York competes in perhaps the most storied NFL title game in history, falling 23–17 in overtime to the visiting Baltimore Colts on December 28.
1963	The Giants lose 14–10 to the host Bears in the league title game on December 29. It is New York's fifth defeat in an NFL Championship Game in six years.

1964	The trading of linebacker Sam Huff and retirements of such players as Frank Gifford and Andy Robustelli kick off an era of bad football for the Giants.
1981	The Giants return to the playoffs for the first time in 18 years and beat the Eagles in Philadelphia, 27–21 on December 27.
1983	Bill Parcells is promoted from defensive coordinator to head coach. After a poor season in 1983, the Giants become a perennial title contender.
1987	The Giants win their first Super Bowl with a 39–20 defeat of the Denver Broncos on January 25.
1991	The Giants win their second Super Bowl in a five-season span, edging the Buffalo Bills 20–19 on January 27. Parcells retires as coach, handing over the job to offensive coordinator Ray Handley.
2001	The Giants make their third Super Bowl appearance. But they fall 34–7 to the Baltimore Ravens on January 28.
2004	Strict Tom Coughlin is hired as coach. He is criticized after a 6–10 season.
2008	The Giants stun the previously unbeaten New England Patriots on February 3 to win their third Super Bowl in four tries, 17–14.
2009	Host New York is upset 23–11 by the Philadelphia Eagles in a divisional playoff game on January 11.

QUICK STATS

FRANCHISE HISTORY
1925–

SUPER BOWLS
(wins in bold)
1986 (XXI), **1990 (XXV)**, 2000
(XXXV), **2007 (XLII)**

NFL CHAMPIONSHIP GAMES
(1933–69; wins in bold)
1933, **1934**, 1935, **1938**, 1939, 1941,
1944, 1946, **1956**, 1958, 1959, 1961,
1962, 1963

NFC CHAMPIONSHIP GAMES
(since 1970 AFL-NFL merger)
1986, 1990, 2000, 2007

DIVISION CHAMPIONSHIPS
(since 1970 AFL-NFL merger)
1986, 1989, 1990, 1997, 2000, 2005,
2008

KEY PLAYERS
(position, seasons with team)
Tiki Barber (RB, 1997–2006)
Roosevelt Brown (OT, 1953–65)
Harry Carson (LB, 1976–88)
Frank Gifford (RB; 1952–60,
    1962–64)
Mel Hein (C, 1931–45)
Sam Huff (LB, 1956–63)
Eli Manning (QB, 2004–)
Andy Robustelli (DE, 1956–64)
Phil Simms (QB, 1979–93)
Michael Strahan (DE, 1993–2007)
Lawrence Taylor (LB, 1981–93)
Amani Toomer (WR, 1996–2008)
Emlen Tunnell (DB, 1948–58)

KEY COACHES
Tom Coughlin (2004–):
    55–41–0; 4–3 (playoffs)
Steve Owen (1931–53):
    151–100–17; 2–8 (playoffs)
Bill Parcells (1983–90):
    77–49–1; 8–3 (playoffs)

HOME FIELDS
New Meadowlands Stadium (2010–)
Giants Stadium (1976–2009)
Shea Stadium (1975)
Yale Bowl (1973–74)
Yankee Stadium (1956–73)
Polo Grounds (1925–55)

* All statistics through 2009 season

Former Giants running back Frank Gifford and quarterback Phil Simms enjoyed highly successful football broadcasting careers after retirement.

"Winning a championship is bigger than that. It's not a payback or a 'Look at me now' situation. It's a great thing for yourself, but also for your teammates, your ownership, everybody. It's too big of a thing, too important of a thing to give a remark or a comeback."
—Giants quarterback Eli Manning, on answering his critics after leading the team to victory in the Super Bowl in February 2008

To win an NFL Most Valuable Player award as an offensive lineman is unheard of in this era of football. But Giants center Mel Hein accomplished the feat in leading the team to a league championship in 1938. Hein set a team record, which has since been matched by quarterback Phil Simms, by playing 15 seasons for the Giants. Hein was an All-NFL selection eight times after the team bid just $150 for his services coming out of college. He never missed a game in high school, college, or professional football. He was placed into the Pro Football Hall of Fame in 1963.

Which quarterback owned the Giants' single-season record for passing yards through 2009? Phil Simms? Eli Manning? Fran Tarkenton? Y. A. Tittle? No, it was Kerry Collins. Collins, who helped the 2000 Giants into the Super Bowl, threw for 4,073 yards in 2002.

GLOSSARY

alignment

The way players are arranged in positions on the field.

attendance

The number of fans at a game or the total number of fans attending games in a season.

berth

A place, spot, or position, such as in the NFL playoffs.

contract

A binding agreement about, for example, years of commitment by a football player in exchange for a given salary.

draft

A system used by professional sports leagues to select new players in order to spread incoming talent among all teams.

franchise

An entire sports organization, including the players, coaches, and staff.

hall of fame

A place built to honor noteworthy achievements by athletes in their respective sports.

innovative

Being creative in doing things a new way, generally with positive results.

Pro Bowl

A game after the regular season in which the top players from the AFC play against the top players from the NFC.

rookie

A first-year professional athlete.

roster

The players as a whole on a football team.

showdown

A long-anticipated battle between two good or great players or teams.

specialization

In football, playing only one position.

FOR MORE INFORMATION

Further Reading

Daily News. *Blue Miracle: New York Giants 2008 Super Bowl Champions.* New York: Sports Publishing, Inc. 2008.

Freedman, Lew, and Pat Summerall. *New York Giants: The Complete Illustrated History*. Minneapolis, MN: MVP Books, 2009.

Vacchiano, Ralph. *Eli Manning: The Making of a Quarterback*. New York: Skyhorse Publishing, 2008.

Web Links

To learn more about the New York Giants, visit ABDO Publishing Company online at **www.abdopublishing.com**. Web sites about the Giants are featured on our Book Links page. These links are routinely monitored and updated to provide the most current information available.

Places to Visit

New Meadowlands Stadium
50 State Route 120
East Rutherford, NJ 07073
201-935-8111
www.newmeadowlandsstadium.com
This 82,000-seat stadium is the new home of the Giants starting in the 2010 season.

Pro Football Hall of Fame
2121 George Halas Drive Northwest
Canton, OH 44708
330-456-8207
www.profootballhof.com
This hall of fame and museum highlights the greatest players and moments in the history of the National Football League. As of 2010, 27 people affiliated with the Giants—including Frank Gifford, Sam Huff, and Lawrence Taylor—had been enshrined.

Timex Performance Center
50 State Route 120
East Rutherford, NJ 07073
www.giants.com/news/headlines/story.asp?story_id=37746
This complex opened in 2009 and serves as the Giants' practice facility and corporate headquarters.

INDEX

About the Author

Marty Gitlin is a freelance writer based in Cleveland, Ohio. He has written more than 25 educational books. Gitlin has won more than 45 awards during his 25 years as a writer, including first place for general excellence from the Associated Press. He lives with his wife and three children.